Positive Affirmations

Positive Thinking to Boost Your Self-Love, Success, Health and Happiness, Free Yourself From Negative Self-Talk and Experience the Rich Life You Deserve

JBC Empower Press

JBCEmpowerPress.com

Copyright ©2022 by JBC Empower Press

Your Thank You Gift

As a thank you for reading this book, we'd like to offer you this uplifting companion gift.

24 Positive Affirmation Cards

These colorful 3-inch square printable cards are perfect for journals, planners and vision boards. You can post them on your mirror, desk or anywhere you will see them daily. Share them with friends and loved ones!

Get yours now by visiting **JBCEmpowerPress.com** and joining our email list. You will receive a link to download your gift right away. You'll also receive periodic updates with inspiring affirmations and more fun giveaways. You can unsubscribe from the list at any time.

Get your gift now at JBCEmpowerPress.com

Table of Contents

Introduction

You are amazing

I know this is 100% true.

I know that you, as an amazing human being, have unique gifts and experiences and incredible abilities to grow and succeed.

What's most important, of course, is that *you* know this is true... with every part of your amazing conscious *and* unconscious mind.

This book exists for you

It exists so you will know, with *100% of your amazing brain*, just how amazing you are.

It exists to train your amazing brain, using *a wealth of powerful, positive affirmations*, to embrace how amazing and capable you are.

To feed your mind daily with powerful positive thoughts and *replace hurtful negative thoughts*.

To create such a strong habit of positive self-talk that *you do it without even thinking about it*... as naturally as breathing.

This book exists to help you receive and achieve all the love, success, health and happiness you deserve!

Are you ready to get started? If so, please do! Just start reading or listening to the first chapter or skip to another topic that calls to you right now. You will find a clear list of specific topics in the Table of Contents to guide you.

Or, if you want to learn more about what positive affirmations are and how they work, or you want tips on how to use them daily, that's great too! Please continue this Introduction chapter.

What Are Positive Affirmations?

Positive affirmations are personal statements that encourage positive beliefs and actions. For example:

- I am amazing.

- I am loved.

- I deserve happiness.

- All I need to succeed is within me.

- I am strong.

- My body is a gift.

- I am confident.

- What I'm feeling is unpleasant, and I will get through it.

- I am kind to others and myself.

- I have the strength to overcome this challenge.

- My mistakes are proof that I am trying.

- Accepting help is a sign of strength.

- I am beautiful, inside and out.

This book gives you a rich collection of positive affirmations to strengthen your beliefs about yourself and encourage new positive beliefs and actions in all areas of your life.

How Positive Affirmations Work

The benefits of positive affirmations can feel magical! But there is real science behind them. *All* humans are born with a tendency to react more strongly to negative signs and events than positive ones. Millions of years ago, when early humans were running from predators, this was a very good thing! When danger *really is* around every corner, fearing the worst is a powerful survival instinct.

Of course, evolutionary change takes centuries. Does that mean you are stuck with a negative attitude? Absolutely not!

Science shows that our amazing brains and thought pathways are *not* set in stone. They are flexible and changeable, and *you* have the power to shape them to your advantage. Scientists have used magnetic resonance imaging (MRI) to see the effects that positive affirmations have on our brains. When you feed your brain positive statements, the parts that process happiness literally light up! Studies also show that practicing positive affirmations can reduce harmful stress and increase motivation and resilience.

You have the power to rewire your own brain for more positivity

This is great news, because today, some of the biggest threats we face to our happiness and success come not from saber-toothed tigers, but from within.

Do you beat yourself up with negative self-talk? Is there a nagging voice in your head saying things like...

- You're not good at this.

- You're going to fail again.

- You'll never be as successful as they are.

- You'll never be as beautiful as she is.

- Why do you deserve happiness?

- Why bother trying?

If so, you are not alone! You, too, can rewire your amazing brain for more confidence, happiness and success.

How to Make Positive Affirmations Part of Your Day

Practice makes progress. To help you make positive thinking as automatic as breathing, you need to practice it on a regular basis. Fortunately, this is easy to do and feels good as well!

If you have the print version of this book, you can read affirmations. If you have the audiobook, you can listen to them. With both versions, of course, you have the best of both worlds!

Trying even just one of these suggestions a day will help you build a strong habit of believing in yourself and your abilities and developing new ones:

Make them part of your routine

- Read or listen to affirmations when you wake up to start your day on a positive note.

- Pick an affirmation to use as a prompt for journaling.

- Write one on a sticky note and put it on your mirror, refrigerator, desk, or other places where you will see it often.

- Write one affirmation each day in your calendar to give you a lift and something to look back on.

- Listen to affirmations on your way to work or school or while doing errands.

- Listen to affirmations while you do chores or take a walk.

- Read or listen to affirmations with your favorite beverage when you need a relaxing or uplifting break.

- Listen to affirmations in the background while you meditate or do yoga.

- Read or listen to affirmations before bed or listen as you drift off to sleep.

Use them to face tough challenges

Positive affirmations are very helpful when you are preparing for anything you consider challenging, like a test, job interview, meeting, game, performance, project, or social event. They are also a healthy tool for coping with upsetting events, big and little disappointments, difficult people and much more.

Share them

Sharing positive affirmations is another great way to practice them. The lucky recipient feels good and so do you! Try texting one to a friend or putting a note in the lunch or bag of a loved one.

There are so many enjoyable ways to practice positive affirmations — you will surely come up with your own favorites!

How to use this book

This book was made for *you*. It is organized so that you can easily get what you need, when you need it most. So, start at the beginning or use the Table of Contents to skip around as much as you like.

This book will be there when you need it — whether that's to start your day, or deal with a tough situation, or relax at the end of the day, or *any* time you want to feed your mind with positivity! Every time you read or listen to *even one* positive affirmation in this book, you are strengthening your habit of positive thinking.

Congratulations on taking this big step toward all the love, success, health and happiness you deserve!

References (Introduction)

Cleveland Clinic. (2021, July 12). Do Positive affirmations Work? What Experts Say: A Psychologist Explains What Affirmations Can Do for Your Mental State. Health Essentials. Retrieved January 10, 2022, from https://health.clevelandclinic.org/do-positive-affirmations-work/

Moore, C. P. (2021, December 8). Positive Daily Affirmations: Is There Science Behind It? PositivePsychology.Com. Retrieved January 10, 2022, from https://positivepsychology.com/daily-affirmations/

Rubin, Z., MD. (2020, June 26). Focus On The Positive: The Science Behind Affirmations And How To Make Them Work For You. Wild Lilac Wellness. Retrieved January 10, 2022, from https://www.wildlilacwellness.com/blog-1/focus-on-the-positive-the-science-behind-affirmations-and-how-to-make-them-work-for-you

Chapter 1:

Affirmations for Self-Love and Love

Love is powerful. Without love, we would be incapable of happiness. Love can also be challenging. Sometimes it can be hard not only to love others but also ourselves. It's time to speak love into existence!

Self-Love and Self-Esteem

1. I am amazing.

2. I am beautiful.

3. I am loved.

4. I am wanted and needed.

5. I am doing my best and my best is enough.

6. If someone hurts me, that is a reflection on them and not me.

7. I am strong.

8. Beating myself up for everything I perceive that I have done wrong isn't going to help me.

9. I am confident.

10. I am gifted with amazing ability.

11. I am a force to be reckoned with.

12. I carry my own power.

13. I look stunning today.

14. I can take on the world.

15. I work hard and do my best every single day.

16. I let go of any self-doubt that plagues my mind.

17. I am independent.

18. My body looks perfect.

19. I don't have to change what I look like to please others.

20. I feel good in my body.

21. Self-hate won't make me feel better.

22. Loving myself brings me joy.

23. I deserve a break.

24. When I need a break, I take one.

25. Perfection is an illusion, and not one I am expected to fulfill.

26. Tonight, I will make time to relax.

27. I will let go of the worry as soon as I leave work.

28. I will leave my work responsibilities at work.

29. I am a human being, and I need to care for myself as such.

30. Having things to do is not an excuse to not practice self-care.

31. I will answer any needs that my body has.

32. If I need time to heal, I will give myself the room to do so.

33. In practicing self-care, I will practice forgiveness.

34.
    I forgive myself for any past mistakes I have made, and I resolve to not let them rule my future.

35. My best might look different from one day to the next, and that is okay.

36. I did my best today.

37. Occasional procrastination is still self-care.

38. Life is always full of projects, but self-care during allthose times matters a lot.

39. I am worthy.

40. I do not need to work to be worthy.

41. I do not need to be perfect to be worthy.

42. I do not have to lose weight to be worthy.

43. My past does not make me unworthy.

44. I don't have to love a certain person or gender to be worthy.

45. I don't have to conform to stereotypes to feel worthy.

46. I am not obligated to hold up others' expectations of me. I am worthy, regardless.

47. How much money I have does not define my worth.

48. My grades do not define my worth.

49. My talents do not define my worth.

50. I will stop basing my worth on frivolous things.

51. I accept who I am.

52. I accept who I love.

53. I accept my talents.

54. I accept that while I might not be good at some things, I am great at others.

55. I accept my body.

56. I accept my mind.

57. I accept and love others.

58. I can accept that there are negative aspects of me, just like there are positive ones.

59. I can accept that the future might be different than what I have imagined, but it is still going to be great.

60. I accept myself and all my unique traits.

61. I deserve the acceptance of others.

62. I do not need to change for others to accept me.

63. I accept that there are some things in life that I won't be able to change.

64. I believe in myself.

65. I can take on big things.

66. I am going places in life.

67. Doors are going to open for me, and I will walk through them.

68. I will stand up for myself and what I believe in.

69. I am strong enough to get past this obstacle.

70. My confidence, by itself, has the power to take me very far in life.

71. Using the confidence I have in myself, I can inspire others to be great!

72. I can go forth and do amazing things in this life.

73. I trust my instincts, especially when they are telling me that I am in a bad situation.

74. I have the power to say no, and I trust myself enough to know when to do so.

75. I trust myself enough to choose the right path.

76. I trust myself and I know when it is time to say yes.

77. If something scares but excites me, I trust myself to try it and see if it's something I enjoy.

78. I trust what I know to be true about myself, and not what other negative perceptions around me say.

79. If I know it's too much, I will say no.

80. I have the right to have healthy boundaries both for myself and for others around me.

81. I deserve to have the peace that boundaries can bring to my life.

82. I am ready to accept the amazing things that come with boundaries.

83. When I need to set boundaries with others, I will tellthem firmly but calmly, and I will not back down.

84. My boundaries are a safe haven for me.

85. I will not give in to pressure when it comes to my boundaries.

86. If I catch myself breaking my personal boundaries, I will stop.

87. It is not okay for someone to ask me to violate my boundaries, even if it is just once.

88. Just because I let someone break a boundary oncedoesn't mean I have to let them do it again.

89. It is okay to set boundaries with loved ones.

90. Boundaries are healthy.

91. By setting boundaries, I am setting myself up for success.

92. I release myself of self-loathing.

93. I permit myself to let go of guilt.

94. I have made peace with my past.

95. My happiness comes from myself and not others.

96. I am in control of my life.

97. I will follow my intuition.

98. I do not need to seek validation from others.

99. I love myself, no matter the circumstance.

100. I love who I am even on my worst days.

101. If I am having a bad day, I stop and remind myself that it isn't all my fault. I am still capable of self-love.

102. I love myself, regardless of my height, weight, or health.

103. My productivity does not determine how much I love myself.

104. I am not defined by how much I do for others.

105. I will not let others define me by the amount of work I didn't get done during that time.

106. I cannot do my best work if I don't love myself.

107. If I don't love myself, my work will never be good enough for me.

108. My work will shine when I love myself.

109. My self-love will translate into my daily activities andprove that I am capable of great things.

110. By practicing self-love, I am unlocking my true potential.

111. I practice self-love by giving myself gifts.

112. I can practice self-love by eating three meals a dayand ensuring that I'm getting the nutrients I need from them.

113. I can practice self-love by drinking water every day.

114. I can practice self-love with exercise today.

115. I can practice self-love by taking a nap.

116. I can't expect from others what I cannot do for myself.

117. I am deserving of love, both from others and myself.

118. I love myself through my thoughts and my actions.

119. I love myself enough to say no when I know that I need to.

120. My love for myself inspires others to think positively.

121. My love for myself will bring me the respect of others.

122. My love for myself extends beyond the activities I fill my life with.

123. My love for myself is letting me heal.

124. My self-love makes me powerful.

125. I recognize myself as a powerful force to be reckoned with.

126. I let my love for myself foster a sense of calm, power,and love.

127. My love for myself will tell me when I need to relax, and I will not ignore it.

Love and Relationships

Love and Attracting Love

1. I am surrounded by love.

2. I will find love wherever I go.

3. I can draw love to me.

4. I love myself as a person.

5. Because I love myself, I will inspire love from others.

6. I deserve love.

7. I accept love from others.

8. The love I receive helps me grow every day.

9. My confidence will help me to attract love.

10. I will find love with the right people.

11. I will discover love when I look.

12. My personality will attract love.

13. The love I attract will be positive.

14. I only need to be myself to attract love.

15. I can attract love.

16. I am worthy of having all the love and support the world has to offer.

17. The love I have for others will never fade.

18. I will love, even when things are tough.

19. I will receive the support offered by those I love.

20. The love I have to both give and receive is infinite.

21. I am blessed with a universe of love.

Family

1. My family and I love each other, even if we don't alwaysget along.

2. It's okay to set boundaries with my family.

3. If my family disrespects me or my boundaries, that is a reflection upon them and not me.

4. I am not a bad person for setting rules or boundariesand deciding to enforce them.

5. I cannot control how my family acts; I can only control my own reactions.

6. The relationship between myself and my familygrows stronger each day.

7. I am grateful for each member of my family, no matter how difficult of a past we might have had before.

8. I can forgive my family for past mistakes, but I don't haveto forget them.

9. I am thankful for the role my family plays in my life.

10. I give thanks to my family.

11. I am a source of delight for my family.

12. I desire to maintain a healthy relationship with my family.

13. My family and I will build each other up. We do not desire to tear each other down.

14. Family drama doesn't matter in the long run. Only our love for each other remains in the end.

15. I am aware of the needs my family has.

16. I only speak of love and not hate to my family members.

17. I am allowed to let my needs come before my family's wants.

18. If my family is a found family rather than a blood family, it is still just as valid.

19. My family inspires me to be a good person.

20. My friends can be part of my family too.

21. If there is toxicity in my family, I can let it go.

Friends

1. I attract amazing friends.

2. I am easy to make friends with.

3. My friends don't expect me to be perfect.

4. My friends and I are there for each other during tough times.

5. I can turn to my friends when I have a bad day.

6. My friends and I don't have to see each other every day to be close.

7. My friends are like family to me.

8. I am awed at how wonderful my friends can be.

9. I will make time for my friends.

10. Visiting with friends can be self-care.

11. There is a strong foundation of trust in my friendships.

12. My friends and I might have varying interests, and that is okay.

13. I can be my full self with my friends. I do not have tohide anything about myself.

14. I can make friends easily when I want to.

15. Making friends is worthwhile.

16. I am open to making new friends.

17. I know my friends on a personal level.

18. My friends are good people to have in my life.

19. My friends and I have boundaries with each other that everyone respects.

20. I am grateful for these wonderful people.

21. I feel confident with both old and new friends.

22. My friends and I are perfect for each other.

23. I love and cherish each of my friends.

24. My friends inspire kindness, happiness, and warmth in me.

25. My friends and I will always be there for each other.

26. I'm grateful that my friends and I are close.

27. Having a family with friends is amazing.

28. Whether or not we grow apart, I will always rememberthese wonderful people.

Healthy Relationships

1. My relationship makes me feel happy.

2. My partner and I deserve love.

3. I deserve a healthy, long relationship, and so does my partner.

4. I am in a committed relationship filled with love and strength.

5. I love my partner a little more every single day.

6. I accept that my partner and I both have weaknesses   thatwe bring into our relationship.

7. I give my relationship the time and attention it deserves.

8. My relationship has healthy and well-communicated boundaries.

9. I support my partner's ambitions and dreams, just   asthey support mine.

10. My partner and I have healthy disputes, and that is okay.

11. Whenever I am with my partner, I feel as though I am safe and comfortable.

12. I am content in my relationship.

13. My partner's love for me is stronger than any fight we have had or will have, and my love for them is just as strong.

14. My partner does things for me, and for that I am grateful.

15. My partner and I are strong both in our relationshipand outside of it.

16. My partner and I healthily rely on each other.

17. I respect my partner's boundaries and ask for clarification if I need it.

18. My flaws are not looked down upon in my relationship.

19. My partner helps me overcome hurdles in my life.

20. My partner is emotionally supportive of me.

21. I feel comfortable sharing my thoughts, problems, and troubles with my partner.

22. My partner and I always respect each other's privacy.

23. I am my true self when I am with my partner.

24. My partner is someone I would choose in another life as well as this one.

25. My partner and I value our relationship with each other, as well as those around us.

26. My partner and I compliment and complete each other.

27. I don't expect perfection from my relationship. I understand that some days it won't be so peaceful.

28. I want to improve on my core self for this relationship.

29. I can be a better person in my relationship without changing fundamental parts of who I am.

30. When either my partner or myself find success, we are very happy for the other person.

Chapter 2:

Affirmations for Happiness

Happiness, for most of us, is technically a choice, but it isn't an easy one to make. Our daily lives often have us stressed and tired. In those moments, it can be hard to say that happiness is what you're going to do that day.

These affirmations are great to repeat to yourself every day. They are also good if you are struggling on a particular day or just need some good vibes to guide you.

Happiness for Myself and Others

1. I am going to have a good day today.

2. I will be positive today.

3. Every single day, I have the goal to love myself even more.

4. I choose joy.

5. I bring joy and happiness to others.

6. I will do something kind for someone today.

7. I am deserving of kindness.

8. While it is true that others can take advantage of my kindness, it is still worth practicing.

9. Practicing kindness can bring happiness.

10. Kindness can be far-reaching.

11. By committing an act of kindness, I inspire everyonearound me to be kind.

12. By practicing kindness, I am spreading love.

13. I can stand up for myself and others.

14. Kindness can open anyone's heart.

15. My kindness can help others see good in the world.

16. By practicing kindness, I am a part of that good.

17. I will inspire others to be positive today.

18. I am positive that I can achieve great things.

19. By being a positive person, I will have better outcomes.

20. I am capable of being positive about my abilities, evenwhen I'm struggling.

21. I give myself permission to view myself positively.

22. I give myself permission to look at my body in a positive light.

23. I look good today.

24. I set the tone for a positive day today.

25. There isn't anyone else out there who is like me.

26. I am successful.

27. I don't need to change myself in any way.

28. I am of value, both to myself and to others.

29. I surround myself with positivity.

30. I am liked and admired.

31. I have good health.

32. I can express who I really am.

33. I am becoming a better person every day.

34. I carry inner beauty with me.

35. My great sense of self-worth carries me through the day.

36. There are opportunities out there for me that I will go after.

37. I will share the happiness of a new morning witheveryone today.

38. I will continue to engage my mind as much as I desire.

39. I am strong.

40. I can overcome any obstacle that comes my way.

41. One bad event will not ruin my whole day.

42. Even if yesterday had bad parts, today has the power tobe great.

43. I look forward to today.

44. I will take the challenges of the day in stride.

45. I have people around me to get me through the tough days.

46. When the day seems like it will be harder, I will take it in stride and not let it get to me.

47. When I have had a bad day, I will practice self-care and relax. I won't carry the negative energy into tomorrow.

48. I permit myself to lean into others for support when I need it.

49. I accept that if something didn't work out, I gave it my best and it wasn't meant to be.

50. It is okay to admit it when I'm struggling, even if it's just to myself.

51. I give myself permission to be gentle with myself.

52. I understand that not every day will be a good one, and I am allowed to have those bad days.

53. I can face uncertainty with confidence.

54. My resilience can be an example to others who are struggling.

55. I will not let someone talk or walk over me today.

56. I do not need to earn basic respect from others.

57. Nothing is completely out of reach for me.

58. I am perfectly capable of getting everything I want in life.

59. Every day I am contributing to the amazing beauty of the world and those contributions are appreciated.

60. My belief in myself is the most important thing to me.

61. I will face today with energy, enthusiasm, and happiness.

62. I refuse to let self-doubt get to me today.

63. I will not allow negative thoughts to control me today.

64. If I find something that makes me happy, I will explore that happiness.

65. I am the one person who can find the answers I amlooking for.

66. Every day, I make progress toward my goals.

67. I have goals and dreams that I will make a reality.

68. It's okay if I experience a setback.

69. Even small steps can lead to big progress.

70. It's okay if my future goals are small. What matters is thatI realize them.

71. I give myself permission to redo my goals if they nolonger serve me.

72. I permit myself to cut out things that do not serve me or my goals.

73. My goals matter whether they are short-term or long-term.

74. Daily progress matters just as much as long-term progress.

75. I will nurture my happiness by doing some self-care every day.

76. Nothing will stop me from achieving the dreams I havefor myself.

77. I have everything that I need to succeed in life.

78. I choose to be confident and to take on the day.

79. My top priority today is to be happy with my work.

80. I accept the good things that I have in life.

81. I greet the day with peace in my heart.

82. I am filled with kindness and happiness today.

83. I like who I am.

84. Today will be full of great adventures.

85. I will pursue new opportunities.

86. I will spread happiness to someone I work with today.

87. I will find joy in the small moments today.

88. I will replace the thoughts that may bring me downwith happier, lively thoughts.

89. I will trade toxic energy for joy and love.

90. I am happier today than I was yesterday.

91. Every day, I have a new and better reason to be happy.

92. I desire to feel joy today.

93. I will let others bring their joy to me.

94. I am overflowing with joy that I will share with theworld today.

95. I have a right to happiness.

96. No one can take away my happiness.

Self-Confidence

1. I can do this.

2. I will overcome my fears.

3. My self-doubt does not govern me.

4. I have everything I need to succeed today.

5. I can do great things with my mind.

6. I choose to be confident today.

7. I look amazing.

8. My body is perfect in every way.

9. I am who I need to be, and I am where I need to be.

10. I have what it takes to be an amazing and successful person.

11. I will not let others' perceptions of me get in my way.

12. I am in charge of my future.

13. I am growing as a person every single day.

14. I am becoming my best self.

15. I cannot wait to meet my future self.

16. I will walk with confidence.

17. I will speak with confidence in my tone.

18. I will not back down from what I know is right.

19. I will not let others try to steal my confidence.

20. I have power thanks to my confidence.

21. I love myself and I draw my confidence from this love.

22. I believe in myself.

23. All areas of my life are influenced by love.

24. My confidence in myself and my love for others will enable me to stand up for them and for what is right.

25. I can express myself with ease.

26. Today, I will win.

27. Today, I will get what I want.

28. I am loved and accepted... by myself.

29. I refuse to be crushed by self-doubt.

30. I accept the natural confidence that has been gifted to me.

31. I allow positive energy to flow through me.

32. I am capable of great things.

33. I banish the negative from my mind.

34. I will not let others' negativity harm me.

35. I will remain a positive force in the world, no matterwhat happens.

36. I think positively, no matter the situation.

37. I am intelligent.

38. I am graceful.

39. I am having fun.

40. I am successful and happy with my life right now.

41. Right now, I am only at the beginning of my journey.

42. I am going to follow my dreams.

43. Everything will come together.

44. I have optimistic thoughts about the future.

45. This is my reality, and I may shape it how I please.

46. I dictate how life happens for me.

47. My work life is richly rewarded.

48. I deserve to have an amazing job.

49. I have strength and clarity available to me today.

50. Thinking positively has the power to transform the lives of myself and others.

51. I can create my reality to be whatever I please.

52. I have the right to high self-esteem. Nobody should be telling me otherwise.

53. I am valued beyond measure.

54. I look in the mirror every day and remind myself that I am beautiful!

55. I am doing good things today.

56. No one can hold me back from my success.

57. I am whole and complete.

58. I recognize my strengths.

59. I can get anything I want in life.

60. I am in a good place right now.

61. I can express my true self easily.

62. I am proud of who I am.

63. I work toward amazing goals.

64. I am working toward the life I desire.

65. I am unbeatable.

66. I will say no when I need to, without feeling bad or guilty.

67. Sometimes, it's enough to just focus on the next stepahead, rather than the entire path.

68. My authentic self is enough.

69. I will not be someone else when I enter the world.

70. I will face my fears with determination.

71. I understand that I cannot help others unless I take careof myself.

72.
    I have the courage to face people and situations that hav e wronged me.

73. I will stand up to the people that hurt me and takemy confidence back.

74. I am a refreshed and amazing human being.

75. I am a warrior, fighting for good things.

76. I make a habit of starting each day with a fresh perspective.

77. I make a habit of walking to work with confidence in my step.

78. I make it a habit to put my needs first.

79. I make it a habit to practice confidence every day.

80. Every day brings me closer to what I want.

81. Nothing must be perfect. It just has to be better than yesterday.

82. I set my priorities each day. If something interferes with these priorities, then I let it go.

83. Others' opinions of the path I am on don't matter, onlymy own.

84. I know that my journey to ideal success has obstacles, and I know that I am built to overcome them.

85. I am growing in esteem each day.

86. I am improving with each day.

87. My ideas are good ones, and they will take me far in life.

88. I can achieve great things.

89. My best is what I can give, and it is enough.

90. The people around me are there to inspire me tomove forward.

91. IfI need something, I can easily ask for it.

92. I can backtrack to take the steps I need to ensure that I am on the right trail.

93. I trust myself completely.

94. I respect who I am.

95. I am healthy.

Gratitude

1. I am grateful for the new day.

2. I am grateful for the sunshine that a day brings so that I can experience the warmth.

3. I am grateful for rain and water.

4. I am grateful to have woken up and to be alive today.

5. I am grateful for the love in my life.

6. There is power in being grateful for the small things in the universe.

7. I will not take things for granted.

8. I am grateful that I am healthy enough to get out of bed today.

9. I am grateful for the food that I have.

10. I will thank someone today, to spread gratitude.

11. I accept my gifts with thanks.

12. There are many things to be grateful for, even in the toughest of times.

13. By practicing gratitude, I will become more mindful.

14. By practicing gratitude, I will become more appreciative of the things I have, and I will not take anything for granted.

15. I will always ensure that the things around me are taken care of.

16. My gratitude will inspire kindness and happiness in others.

17. I am selfless.

18. I have worked hard for the things around me.

19. My work is appreciated.

20. I am grateful that there is kindness in the world.

21. I am grateful to live somewhere where I can express myself and pass on the joy of living.

22. I am grateful that life decided to give me a chance to see today.

23. I am grateful for the air that I can breathe.

24. On days where things seem to be going wrong, I am still grateful for those things that go right.

25. I am grateful for my family.

26. I am grateful for my significant other.

27. I am grateful for my friends.

28. I express the gratitude I have for the world.

29. I know that being grateful doesn't mean I can't be upset.

30. I am grateful for a chance to fulfill my dreams today.

31. I am grateful that I can freely walk to where I need to be today.

32. I am grateful to feel the warmth of the sun against my face.

33. I am grateful that I exist in a world of love and happiness.

34. I find grace in what I have, as I strive to work toward bigger goals.

35. I am grateful to the mentors that I have had along the way.

36. I am grateful for the beauty I possess.

37. I am grateful to hold confidence and power in my life.

38. I am grateful that there is a future out there for me.

39. I am grateful for my current spot in life.

40. I am grateful to have a roof over my head.

41. I am grateful that I can take care of myself.

42. I am grateful that I can go into the world and make an impact on it.

43. I am grateful for the flowers, and how beautiful they are.

44. I am grateful for the conveniences that are available to me as a member of the modern world.

45. I am grateful for the education I have been able to receive.

46. I am grateful for the places I have been able to experience throughout my life.

47. I am grateful to be able to feel every emotion that exists on the spectrum.

48. I will not allow my grace to be taken advantage of when it hurts me.

49. I am grateful that I am alive to experience the wonders around me.

50. I am grateful for the places I hold in the hearts of my loved ones.

51. I am grateful for the support I receive from my family each day.

52. I am grateful for the lessons that I have learned from my mistakes.

53. I am grateful for having a body that can do a lot of great things.

54. I am grateful for safety and security.

55. I am grateful to my comfort zone for when I need it, and for the ability to step outside of it when I am ready.

56. I commit to being a grateful person, while I still hold the excitement that the future is upon me and I have every ability to embrace it.

57. I am grateful that my heart is open and able to give others the joy of love.

58. I am grateful that there are people in my life who can love me and support me and my future.

59. I am grateful that I have the freedom to choose who I love.

60. I am grateful for the good that is left in the world.

61. I promise myself that as I head toward my future, I will be grateful for the things I have and the things I gain.

62. I will be grateful for whatever happens in the future.

63. I am grateful for the things and the people that have guided me in this life.

64. I am grateful for the things and the people that have taught me and reminded me about the importance of love.

65. My gratefulness opens my eyes to new opportunities.

66. I am grateful for the transformative moments that I have experienced in life.

67. When I am facing tough times, I will remember to be grateful for the good in life.

68. I am grateful that not everything in this world will be perfect. I accept that the imperfections of the world help me to see the beauty.

69. There are many great things ahead of me that I will embrace.

70. If I come into the situation with an appreciation for the people involved, then I will receive that appreciation back, as well as a good outcome for all involved.

71. In my gratitude, I extend trust in that there is a future for me past these uncertain times.

72. I appreciate the things that this season of life has taught me.

73. I am grateful for this time in my life.

74. I will always do my best to show appreciation for the world around me.

75. I am thankful for the ordinary things of life.

76. My appreciation for ordinary things allows me to look past a normal exterior and uncover the beauty within them.

77. I am grateful for the existence of beaches.

78. I am grateful for the existence of forests and trees.

79. I am grateful for hiking trails and the ability to enjoy nature.

80. No matter what I face in life, I will never stop being grateful.

81. My attitude of being grateful and accepting has brought me new and amazing experiences, including happiness.

82. The feeling of being grateful for even the small things in life has opened my eyes and enabled me to see into the universe.

83. I put my grateful attitude into action.

84. I smile at the people I pass by and inspire them to smile at the next person they see.

85. My example can cause a chain reaction that can go on for miles.

86. My grateful energy provides me and the others around me with a renewed sense of spirit each day.

87. My grateful spirit allows me to be stronger and overcome difficult challenges.

88. My grateful attitude can bring light to an otherwise dark situation.

89. My grateful attitude allows me to take things that are weighing me down and turn them into things that lift me up.

90. I understand that a gesture of gratitude can be as extravagant as buying flowers for someone, or as simple as saying thank you. I commit to at least one gesture of gratitude a day.

91. Today I will walk hand in hand with peace.

92. I am grateful to have a peaceful life.

93. I am grateful to know joy in my life.

94. I am grateful to myself for being as strong as I can be.

95. I am grateful that I can allow myself to relax.

96. I am grateful that this mindset can attract great things in life.

Success

1. I am dedicated to learning new things.

2. Today, I am going to try something new.

3. I will dedicate time to a skill that I want to learn.

4. I understand that while something might not be perfect on the first try, I can always try it again.

5. I understand that I will make mistakes, but I commit to learning from them rather than letting them discourage me.

6. Every time I attempt to do something, I am improving my skills.

7. I have great talents that are waiting to be used.

8. My time is coming, and I bring it closer every day that I put more work into it.

9. I will not stop here.

10. Even if I feel as though I have perfected my craft, I will not stop growing my expertise.

11. When it comes time for me to learn new things, I give it my full attention.

12. I dedicate time every day to learning new things and growing.

13. I know that a big part of succeeding is learning how to do it.

14. There isn't anything I can do right now that would hinder my success. Every step I take is a step forward, no matter what trouble the step might bring.

15. I do not fear failure.

16. Personal growth is a success.

17. To succeed, there may need to be growth in my knowledge or in myself.

18. Every milestone is a reason to celebrate.

19. I am successful in my journey and work.

20. I desire success.

21. By making my desire known, it will come to me.

22. I am worth celebrating.

23. Small success matters just as much.

24. I am fearless in the face of failure.

25. With each failure comes a learning experience that I can use to succeed in the future.

26. With each step I take, I am moving forward in life.

27. I will celebrate the success of others.

28. With my success comes joy.

29. I will not compare my success with others.

30. My big success might look small to others, but thatdoesn't make it any less valid.

31. I will succeed in putting myself first and taking care of myself.

32. If I give effort, no matter what the task is, I will succeed in the end.

33. Success will come to me naturally.

34. I will see a lot of success in my life.

35. Each failure that I experience increases how great my success will be.

36. I will receive an abundance of success.

37. Success flows through me.

38. I am successful because I believe in myself.

39. My drive and passion lead me to be successful.

40. Every time that I succeed, something great is born.

41. I am not failing; I am just finding things that don't work and crossing them off the list.

42. I believe that I have the power to succeed in life.

43. My success will lead me to a great life.

44. My successes in life are numerous, no matter how large or small they might be.

45. I can realize my dreams.

46. If something is treated with importance, then it has agreat chance of success.

47. I treat myself like someone who deserves to succeed.

48. I will not get stuck on the failures.

49. The more I learn and try, the more successful I will become.

50. I will set a routine.

51. I will give myself time to work on my projects.

52. I deserve to have the time to work on my projects.

53. I am smart and I will make good decisions.

54. I am confident.

55. My confidence brings me productivity and success.

56. I will not let failure get the best of me.

57. Failure cannot cloud my judgment.

58. No matter what happens, I won't give up.

59. The opportunities I have are unlimited.

60. I will create amazing things.

61. I spend time discovering interesting and excitingnew information.

62. My decisions are good ones, even if they don't lead where I want them to.

63. I don't have to succeed on major points just to succeed in life.

64. I am oriented toward my life goals.

65. There are great people in my life who want to see me succeed.

66. I am motivated to win in life.

67. I am striving toward my full potential every day.

68. I have the tools I need to overcome the bumps down the road.

69. I choose to let go of the negative thoughts that will keep me from being productive and successful.

70. I chose productivity today.

71. I discover a strength within myself every day.

72. I choose to be positive and to have a positive outlook on my future.

73. I am making a great plan.

74. I will tackle challenges with an open mind, so that Imay succeed in the best possible way.

75. I am grateful for the success in life that I have had thus far.

76. I face each day with confidence, power, and a sense of peace that leads me on a successful path.

77. I am successful when I make positive changes in my life.

78. My health is a success.

79. My freedom to choose things for my life is a success.

80. I will be persistent with what I do.

81. My success will contribute to the world in good ways thatI cannot yet understand.

82. I will persist, even after the toughest of failures hit me.

83. I will ensure that others around me have the tools to succeed.

84. Each day brings new opportunities for my success.

85. I will succeed by eating a healthy meal today.

86. I will succeed by practicing self-care today.

87. I will succeed by being kind today.

88. I am creative.

89. My creativity gives me power.

90. My creativity can give birth to great ideas.

91. The way creativity manifests in me is unique and that means that my ideas are unique.

92. I will use my creativity to generate amazing new ideas.

93. I deserve a chance to use my creative mindset.

94. My unique ideas will help others.

Chapter 3:

Affirmations for Financial Success

While affirmations do not make money magically appear, they can help you increase focus and confidence. You can create positive attitudes about opportunities, abundance, your work ethic, your money skills, and much more. Your attitudes fuel your actions and your results.

Money and Wealth

Abundance and Gratitude

1. I am grateful for what I have.

2. I have abundant resources.

3. Abundance is coming to me.

4. I deserve abundant resources.

5. I am grateful for my work.

6. I am grateful for my ability to provide for myself and my family.

7. I am grateful for the opportunities I have had that have led me to this moment.

8. I seek out opportunity and it leads to abundance.

9. I can seek things that bring me the wealth I need.

10. I am grateful for the many talents that allow me to lead my life.

11. I have enough.

12. The resources I need are on their way to me.

13. I am seeking the path that leads me to where I will receive the life I am dreaming of.

14. I can rely on my instincts to guide me to abundance.

15. I am grateful for the resources the world has to offer.

16. I am grateful that I can follow my ambition.

17. I am surrounded by abundant gifts.

18. I am grateful for the opportunities I receive, and I takefull advantage of them.

19. I have the power to create abundance for myself.

20. I am grateful for the small gifts of life, as they do add up.

21. I am grateful for the opportunity to choose what I want and lead my own way to abundance.

22. I accept the gifts that the universe has given me.

23. I choose to develop my skills.

24. I have many skills that I can use.

25. My gratitude adds to my abundance.

Goals and Action

1. I am committed to my goals.

2. I have written down my goals.

3. I have daily goals that I will reach.

4. I can see my long-term goals.

5. I know the path I must take to meet my goals.

6. My goals are only meant to serve me, and my family. I do not have to validate them to anyone.

7. I have tasks to complete that are a part of my goal.

8. My goals are taking me far in life.

9. I am on track to reach my goals.

10. I have given my goals deadlines so that I stay focused.

11. I spend time working toward my goals every single day.

12. My goals are healthy for me.

13. My goals are possible for me to achieve.

14. My goals give me insight every day.

15. I am acting today to meet my goals.

16. I have a plan that is set in motion.

17. I will meet my deadlines.

18. My goals are the most important thing to me.

19. I am set up for success with my goals.

20. I have set goals that are meaningful to me.

21. My goals will help me succeed in life.

22. I am driven by my goals.

23. Today, I will dedicate time to mapping out my goals.

24. I will set weekly goals to help me achieve my monthly goals.

25. Every step I take is progress for my goals.

Saving and Managing

1. I am responsible with money.

2. I manage my finances well.

3. I know what bills need to be paid.

4. I have a plan for getting everything paid for.

5. I am smart with my assets.

6. I know the steps that I am following are the right ones.

7. I have budgeted only for the money that I have.

8. I do not need borrowed money for my needs.

9. I am doing good with my money.

10. My money is serving me.

11. I am wise with my money.

12. I manage my money well and ensure there is enough room for everything.

13. I stay within my budget.

14. I am realistic with my budget.

15. I ensure that my budget includes expenses for me.

16. I ensure that I am being cared for by my money.

17. I know that if something goes wrong, I have a safety net.

18. I am saving for long-term goals.

19. I have something fun in mind that I am saving for.

20. My budgeting habits help me tremendously.

21. I can set myself up for long-term financial success.

22. I am good at making sure that I have enough money at the end of the week.

23. I can trust myself to make the right financial decisions.

24. Before making a purchase, I know it doesn't interfere with long-term goals.

25. By budgeting now, I know that my future is set.

Sharing and Enjoying

1. My money works for me.

2. I deserve to treat myself.

3. I am grateful for my life's fortune.

4. I am grateful to be able to give to others who are in need.

5. My kindness is far-reaching.

6. I have the power to help others.

7. I can give gifts to others who are in need.

8. I can share time with others.

9. I give myself permission to enjoy the rewards of my work.

10. My money allows me to do more than just survive.

11. My money gives me the freedom to enjoy the delights of life.

12. I share my kindness with others.

13. I have an abundance of resources that I can share, both with myself and others.

14. I am grateful for what I have, and I take the opportunity to help others.

15. My actions in sharing with others have a big impact.

16. My empathy extends into kindness for both myself and others.

17. I am generous.

18. I am helping others in their time of need.

19. I am inspiring the people around me.

20. I have taken care of myself.

21. I am ensuring that others can meet needs of their own.

22. I am inspiring others around me to give to someone in need.

23. I can share my success with others.

24. I can enjoy what I have earned.

25. I am doing great every day.

Success and Motivation

Success Mindset

1. I can do anything I set my mind to.

2. I am confident in the work that I do.

3. I can achieve the goals that have been laid out for me.

4. I do not stop, even when I am faced with failure.

5. I complete the projects on my own when I can and ask for help when I need to.

6. I put my best work into my projects.

7. When an idea fails, I try to learn from it, instead of lettingit discourage me.

8. I work well under pressure.

9. I am meeting all my deadlines.

10. I have plans for completing my projects on time.

11. I know what the next step is in my project, and I am ready to take it.

12. I am doing my best work today.

13. I am disciplined in the approach that I take.

14. I am good at my work.

15. My desire to learn is abundant.

16. If I find something that interests me, I will explore this interest.

17. I refuse to ever let myself be outpaced by technology.

18. I know that even though my project is difficult now, a time will come when I can succeed.

19. I can succeed in what I am doing.

20. I am continually pushing myself to do better.

21. I am focused on getting the best possible results from this project.

22. I have an instinct for success.

23. It is easy for me to succeed at work.

24. I have the tools I need to do the job right.

25. I make consistent progress toward my work every single day.

Self-Confidence and Motivation

1. I can succeed at anything I put my mind to.

2. I am an amazing person and an amazing worker.

3. I am a successful being.

4. My mistakes are not pulling me down. They are merely learning opportunities.

5. I can handle stressful situations with ease.

6. I allow my wisdom to flow as I work to make the best decisions.

7. I focus on clarity as I work so that I can always see thebig picture.

8. I can take on many challenges.

9. I am good at staying balanced when faced with stress.

10. I do not let stressful situations disrupt my productivity.

11. I deserve to succeed in my work.

12. I have a brilliant mind.

13. I am smart and talented.

14. I am a natural leader.

15. I am where I am supposed to be right now.

16. I will go on to complete amazing things.

17. I am doing great work every single day.

18. I am working on my dreams.

19. I am needed by my company.

20. I do amazing work every day.

21. I am learning something new every day.

22. My new knowledge will serve me well when it comesto projects that happen later.

23. I am passionate about what I do.

24. What I do is fulfilling for me.

25. I am moving ahead in life.

Creativity

1. My upcoming project is new and exciting.

2. My ideas for upcoming projects are great.

3. By sharing my new ideas, I could lead to someamazing breakthroughs.

4. Even if one idea fails, I should still try another.

5. All my ideas are good, even the ones that don't work out.

6. I give myself time to brainstorm.

7. I am not afraid to take risks.

8. My creativity gives me and my company a competitive edge.

9. I am smart and capable of creating great things.

10. I take notes, so that I may share my ideas with others.

11. I take advantage of offered help during thebrainstorming process.

12. If my creativity seems to be failing me, I have steps I can take to help my brain get back on track.

13. I give myself permission to look at all the options, eventhe unusual ones.

14. My thinking skills are leading me toward creating amazing things.

15. If one thing doesn't work, I have another idea to try.

16. I am a creator. I make things work.

17. I always envision how my projects could be greater, and what might help them be better.

18. I am a forward thinker.

19. I love my work and the things I make and do there.

20. I accept the gift of creativity that I have.

21. I know the steps I need to take for my idea to be realized.

22. My creativity makes me a valuable contributor.

23. My work has benefited others.

24. I will never let anyone stop me from trying to create new things.

25. I am energized by the things I can create.

Productivity

1. My positivity will lead to productivity today.

2. I will make a plan for accomplishing my projects.

3. I will stick to my deadlines.

4. I will learn how to conquer the small tasks so that I can move on to bigger ones.

5. I will put my effort toward succeeding where it will serveme best.

6. Today, I will get up and I will work.

7. I have goals and I am putting them in motion.

8. I am ready to face any joys or challenges that the jobbrings today.

9. If I start struggling with staying productive, I will pause and let my brain get back into that mindset.

10. I am going to accomplish things today.

11. I am going to do things that make a big difference today.

12. I am going to be on time today.

13. I am engaging the best thinking parts of my brain today.

14. I will not let distractions stop me from being productive today.

15. I can only succeed if I get my work done.

16. I have my tasks laid out for me.

17. I know what I need to get done for today.

18. I keep a to-do list so that I don't get lost in the day.

19. I am doing what I need for me to succeed.

20. I am completing all my work, step by step.

21. My routine is encouraging me to be productive.

22. I have laid distractions aside.

23. I am going to complete my list today.

24. I am moving forward with every step.

25. I know what my priorities are, and I will focus on them first.

Work and Business

Achievement and Resilience

1. I will accomplish the things I have started.

2. I will not let things get in my way.

3. I will not let other projects get in the way of the one I find to be most important.

4. My priorities dictate what I will accomplish first.

5. I know what is most important.

6. I have surrounded myself with people who are helping me meet my goals.

7. I am making choices every day and those are helping guide me to where I need to go.

8. I am succeeding.

9. Success in smaller projects means that success is going to be easy to find in big projects too!

10. I know that some projects require a lot of work, and I am willing to put in that work to see great results.

11. I have generated respect from others, both due to my personality, and my achievement.

12. If something or someone challenges me, I can overcome this challenge.

13. I am focused and determined to get this project completed to the best of my ability.

14. I am doing the work and I'm doing it well.

15. I have a set focus on what I need to complete for this project.

16. I know what steps I am taking today.

17. I prepare myself to work hard every day to achieve thegoals that I want to.

18. I am challenging myself to do better every day.

19. I find happiness in the challenge that work provides.

20. I find passion in my work.

21. I have a focus set on my mission.

22. I am inspiring others around me to do the best w0rk that they can.

23. I am working with my team and coworkers to ensure that the work is being done to the best of our abilities.

24. I will persist in work, even when the project seems to struggle.

25. I can gain satisfaction from a completed project.

26. It makes me happy to know that a completed projectwill benefit others.

27. I have gained respect from my superiors for the work that I do.

28. I am consistently adding value to my workplace everysingle day.

29. I find inspiration in my work.

30. I am inspired by both success and failure.

31. I am doing the right work every day.

32. Challenges are merely opportunities to me.

33. I am motivating myself through my work.

34. The potential for the work I do is unlimited.

35. I am doing things that help me achieve what I want in life.

36. I am standing up to face each challenge.

37. I am excelling at the work I do.

38. I find energy in my success.

39. I can see the success of this project right in front of me.

40. I am at ease, no matter how stressful the situation is.

41. I am encouraged to grow thanks to the environmentaround me.

42. I will finish this project and it will be amazing.

43. I have already done many great things in the past, and Iwill continue to do this.

44. I am determined to do my best work.

45. Even in the face of failure, I can succeed.

46. I am living up to my full potential every day.

47. I am ensuring that I am in my best mindset for work.

48. I take a moment to reflect on my success.

49. I am strong and mighty.

50. My work ethic is steady, and it is helping me succeed.

Recognition and Reward

1. I am recognized for my hard work.

2. I have done an amazing job.

3. I have gained the respect of others thanks to my performance.

4. My work will reap profit for myself and my company.

5. My work is leading me to the life I want to live.

6. I deserve to see the benefits of my work.

7. I am strong for what I have accomplished.

8. I take pride in what I have accomplished.

9. I take a moment to rest after a big success. I have earned it.

10. I recognize that I have done a great job.

11. I know that my best work is in the project.

12. I own my work.

13. I am humble about my accomplishments, but I do notdeny their power.

14. I will continue to do great things.

15. I will see a reward for my work.

16. My work will help others and will find reward in that.

17. My work will be noticed by my superiors.

18. I will use this success to aim for bigger projects, withmore success as a part of them.

19. My work has made me better off.

20. My work can bring financial gain.

21. This success will be carried forward into my next project.

22. This success proves that I can succeed at anything I try to.

23. I will use this success to my advantage. It will not be wasted.

24. This success brings me happiness.

25. My success proves to me that I am on the right track.

26. I am doing my best work right now.

27. I am finding motivation in my success.

28. I am doing fantastic work right now.

29. Because I have done my best, there are many rewards in store for me.

30. Others see me now because I have done great work.

31. My work has added to my confidence.

32. My decisions will lead to more success in the future.

33. I have done a wonderful job in this.

34. This success has added to my ambition to continue my work.

35. This success has brought me immeasurable growth.

36. I have proven to myself that I am doing the right things right now.

37. I have gained a lot of insight from this.

38. I have learned a lot while doing this project.

39. I am learning more and more every single day, andthat knowledge is a gift.

40. I have proven myself to be a capable, hardworking, confident individual.

41. I have made great use of the time I had.

42. I have made great use of the talents I have.

43. Thanks to this success, I am experiencing self-esteem growth.

44. I have just completed something great, and I am proud of it.

45. My success has the power to change my life for the better.

46. I am successful.

47. I have done something new, and I succeeded.

48. This success is bringing me new opportunities.

49. Each failure contributed to the success of this project, andI will remember that.

50. I will take time to reward myself for the amazing work that I have done.

Chapter 4:

Affirmations for Health and Wellness

Let's be honest. Society doesn't prioritize our health. Today, we live in a world where working to the brink is glamorized while having a healthy work-life balance is often painted as lazy. Sometimes, you need to take care of yourself first and ignore those around you that tell you otherwise. These affirmations will help you value and prioritize your health.

Health

Good Choices

1. I will make good choices for my health.

2. If doing something will hurt my health, I will say no.

3. I will get enough sleep tonight. If work tries to get in the way of this, I won't let it.

4. I refuse to let my job or other work have a bad impact on my health.

5. If I need time off for my health, I will take it.

6. I will not let myself be guilted into hurting my health.

7. I will set boundaries that will help in my health.

8. I will be clear with family, friends, coworkers, and bosses about my limits.

9. I am allowed to take breaks.

10. I will not let others take my breaks from me.

11. When my needs aren't met, I will take action to meet them.

12. I know that self-care is vital to my health.

13. I will make sure that I am not overdoing it.

14. I listen to my body when it tells me that I need to take time off.

Exercise

1. I use my workout to relieve stress and anxiety.

2. I will not let work stop me from exercising.

3. I will make it a goal to keep exercise alive in my life.

4. I deserve to be able to make time for exercise.

5. I know that exercise will keep me healthy.

6. Even if my mind protests, I will ensure that I take the time to exercise.

7. I know that there are great benefits to exercising.

8. I don't have to always do big workouts. Ensuring that I am moving and stretching is enough.

9. I will feel better with each day that I exercise.

10. I do not have to join a gym for it to count as exercise.

11. I commit to getting fresh air with some of my exercises.

12. I don't just exercise alone. Friends might come sometimes too.

13. I am excited about my workout today.

14. I want to work out and be healthy.

15. Today, I am going to give my workout my best effort.

16. My body will become stronger with this workout.

17. Today's workout is going to be fulfilling.

18. I have the power to do my exercise to the fullest today.

19. I have the power to do whatever I want for my exercise.

20. Exercise in any form is fun.

21. If I want to go to the gym, I will.

22. If I have access to the gym, I will use that access.

23. I have some go-to exercises.

24. I wake up ready to work out every morning.

25. Every day, I notice that my strength and stamina are increasing.

Strength

1. I deserve to be strong and healthy.

2. I have the strength to say no to things that hurt my health.

3. I have the strength to get out of bed every morning.

4. My willpower will override the voices telling me to breakmy boundaries for them.

5. I will make good choices for my health.

6. I can find strength in what I am doing.

7. When I push myself to be healthy, my body thanks me.

8. I am getting closer to my goals for my health.

9. I feel good about my health right now.

10. I am motivated to take the steps that I need to take.

11. I will continue to seek healthy options.

12. I can break from my healthy patterns for a day withno consequence. I will get back into it the next day.

13. I am choosing to be healthy to increase my happiness.

14. I am choosing to be healthy to increase my productivity.

15. I am choosing to be healthy to live longer.

16. I am choosing to be healthy because it feels good.

17. My mind is strong.

18. My body is strong, and I am working on building it every day.

19. I have health and fitness goals and I am confident about them.

20. I will exercise regularly.

21. I am proud of myself for exercising.

22. My personal fitness increases with exercise.

23. I am dedicating myself to building my strength, fitness,and mind.

24. I am resilient and I can withstand anything.

25. I am taking care of my body by exercising.

26. I am in love with my body.

27. I will not give up on being healthy, even after I reach my goals.

28. I can do this. If I set a goal, I will achieve it.

29. I have made it far in my health journey and I am pumped with energy to continue.

30. Motivation for my health journey comes to me more easily than it ever has.

31. I love the feeling I get after finishing a long workout.

32. The sweat that falls with each workout will releasetoxins. Those will no longer be a part of my body.

33. Every day that I work out, I can see the positive changes in my body.

34. Pushing myself to eat right and work out is strengthening me physically.

35. I am thankful that I have a body that can do the things I want it to do.

36. I want to give my body the healthy inputs it needs.

37. My goal is to take care of myself.

Activity

1. I will eat healthy today.

2. I will get enough sleep today.

3. I will exercise today.

4. I will drink enough water today.

5. I will set up a routine that will allow me to be healthy.

6. I will practice saying no when I need to.

7. I will make sure that I am firm with my boundaries.

8. I will not let myself trade my health for more work.

9. I will ensure that I do my best to remain healthy on thehard days.

10. I accept my good health.

11. I check in with my body and its needs every day.

12. After a workout, I pay attention to how my body feels.

13. I refuse to quit. I will set weekly goals to ensure that quitting is not an option.

14. When I struggle with motivation, I remember my goals.

15. I am committed to eating fruits and vegetables today.

16. My hard work is paying off.

17. I am becoming the best version of myself, physicallyand mentally.

18. While I aim towards my goals, I will not overwork myself.

Wellness

Loving Your Body

1. My body deserves love and support.

2. Weight is only a number.

3. I am happy with what I look like.

4. I look amazing.

5. If I am overweight, I don't need to punish myself.

6. My eyes are beautiful.

7. My hair looks healthy.

8. My skin looks good.

9. I don't have to look like a runway model to be healthy.

10. I understand that the negative perceptions that I have of myself have largely been formed by the media and are not true.

11. I reject the influence of social media and the effect it has on my body.

12. I reject the words of others telling me that my body must look a certain way.

13. I will not let friends or family members makenegative comments about my body.

14. Focusing too much on my appearance will not lead togood health outcomes.

15. My commitment is to my health and not to the scale.

16. I know that the scale isn't really the best measuring tool.

17. Each cell in my body is important to my function.

18. I view my body in a positive way.

19. I lead my body, and I will lead it along a healthy path.

20. I choose to think about my body as being healthy and well, no matter what others say.

21. If I feel that there are steps that I can take to make my body feel even better than it does right now, then I will take those steps.

22. If something in my body needs to change, I know that it will tell me and that I will listen.

23. I am radiant and glowing.

24. I am a healed person.

25. I strive for balance in myself.

26. Every morning, I can wake up and name something that I love about myself.

27. I am a wonderful person.

28. My intelligence is magnificent and inspiring.

29. I love myself.

30. I don't love myself because of false information, but rather the truth that lies within me.

31. I will stay motivated to achieve peace within myself.

32. I will use this body to realize the full potential I have in life.

33. I am in charge of my life and how I see myself.

34. If someone tries to make a negative comment about me, I will not be afraid to stop them.

35. If I say it, and I work for it, it will come true.

36. I have every day of my life ahead of me, and I desire to spend them knowing and loving who I am as a person.

37. I express myself and who I am, no matter what others think.

38. I make conscious choices every day to love and take care of my body.

39. I hold compassion for my body.

40. The size of my heart is not determined by the size of my stomach. My heart is what will make this world a better place.

41. When I think about my future, I am filled with determination to be my best self.

Self-Care

1. I will take time for myself.

2. I trust my body to tell me when everything is okay, and when it isn't.

3. I trust myself to know when it is time to rest.

4. I trust myself to know when I am hungry.

5. I trust myself to know when I am full.

6. I will ignore negative messages.

7. Self-care is essential.

8. Eating right is self-care.

9. I will relax after a long day at work.

10. I am allowed to feel tired.

11. I am allowed to take time to care for myself.

12. Self-care allows me to heal.

13. Self-care will help me deal with the hard problems in my life.

14. Self-care can make my life easier, even if it's just small things.

15. I will do something nice for myself today.

16. There isn't anyone who can dictate what I do as self-care. I am a freethinking person.

17. I relate to my body, and I know when I need to take some time for healing.

18. By practicing self-care, I am nourishing my body and its energy levels.

19. I am intelligent. I know when I have all the energy in the world to get things done, and I know when it is time for me to lay down and take a nap.

20. By practicing self-care, I am giving my body the balance it needs physically, mentally, and emotionally.

21. My body is capable of healing itself.

22. I trust my gut when my body says something is right or wrong.

23. I trust that I know my body.

Fitness

1. Fitness is about more than just working out. I can be fit even if I don't work out every single day.

2. Fitness is not based on the number on the scale.

3. I give my best effort every day

4. I will choose the workouts that are best for my goals.

5. My emotional fitness is important.

6. I maintain my fitness by drinking enough water every day.

7. I maintain my fitness by eating healthy meals every day.

8. I maintain my fitness by making sure the environmentaround me supports my needs.

9. I maintain my fitness by trying new things and experiencing life.

10. By drinking water, I am giving life to myself.

11. I am maintaining my fitness by making sure that I am getting enough sleep every night.

12. I will say yes to being healthy and strong.

13. I will say yes to accepting who I am.

14. I will take care of my emotional health.

15. I have people that I can reach out to when I need help.

16. I will seek people out when I need to.

17. If I need help with my fitness goals, I can get it.

18. I will not let myself refuse help if I am in need.

19. I can help myself by listening to my body.

20. I know where I can find help if I need it.

21. I am seeking balance for myself.

Healing

Emotional Healing

1. My emotional health is important.

2. My emotional health is vital to my success.

3. My emotional health matters to me.

4. I know that my physical and mental health will lag if I don't take care of my emotional health first.

5. I deserve emotional safety.

6. I will face things that have caused me pain.

7. I will overcome fears that have led me to pain.

8. I am worthy of emotional health.

9. My emotional health is significant and healing it willgreatly improve my life.

10. I give myself permission to take the day off when I need to.

11. If someone is hurting my emotional health, I permit myself to cut them out of my life.

12. I give myself permission to feel angry at the personthat harmed my emotional health.

13. I permit myself to experience all the emotions that come along with healing.

14. I give myself permission to get rid of the negativity around me.

15. I love myself, flaws and all.

16. I will love myself for how I am now, even as I worktoward being a better person.

17. I will not hide my feelings.

18. My emotional healing journey starts with myself.

19. I give myself compassion, kindness, love, and patience.

20. I deserve happiness and will always share it with others.

21. I replace the negative thoughts for myself with love.

22. I replace any hate for others I might feel for inner peace.

23. I will face my angry emotions head-on and be at peace.

24. I allow my feelings of agitation to leave me, so that I may be at peace.

25. I will receive compliments peacefully.

26. I am worthy of compliments from others.

27. When someone makes a positive comment about me, I accept it as the truth.

Inner Peace

1. I understand that forgiveness will help me be at peace, and I will forgive as soon as I am ready.

2. I accept the troubling things that lead me to this point.

3. I understand that it's okay to be angry at the world sometimes, but we must not be consumed with this anger.

4. I will take a deep breath if I begin to feel overwhelmed.

5. I will allow myself time away from the screen and the news, as that can sometimes be necessary to build peace within myself.

6. I deserve to feel content, even when the world around me is in chaos.

7. I will add activities, such as meditation, to my day to help me feel more at peace with myself.

8. Being at peace with myself can inspire others who needhelp finding this peace.

9. I am doing okay mentally.

10. I don't have to feel perfect when it comes to my mental health. I am allowed to note that I am facing challenges.

11. I am working toward better mental health every day.

12. I will replace the negative thoughts in my brain with positivity.

13. I am powerful and profound. This power will inspire peace.

14. Today, my strength is with me.

15. Peace and harmony lie within me and are always availableto me.

16. I will choose activities that help give me peace.

17. I will spend some time in nature today.

18. I will spend time meditating or calming my mind today.

19. I deserve respect from others. I will not accept hostility.

Acceptance

1. I accept that some things are beyond my control.

2. I accept that I might have some bad days, and that's okay.

3. I accept that it might be hard for others to understand what it's really like to be me, but I know that it isn't my job to teach them.

4. I accept that there are challenging parts to creating good mental health, and I embrace the fact that I may struggle.

5. I will say goodbye to the negative thoughts in my brain and hello to positivity and energy.

6. I release myself of any toxic elements that were found inmy body.

7. My body is amazing and each cell within knows what needs to be done to heal.

8. I am grateful for the peace and harmony within me every day.

9. I choose to crave only the things that increase my health.

10. I will create good habits in my life.

11. I accept the extra energy of the day.

12. There are people out there who love me, and I accepttheir love.

13. I love and accept myself. I am my favorite person.

14. Just as I inspire peace and kindness in others, I let them inspire peace and kindness in me.

15. I am comforted by the peace that now exists.

Letting Go

1. I choose to let go of what is holding me back.

2. I am choosing to focus on my mental well-being.

3. I discard anything fake I have presented about myself. I give myself permission to be my true self.

4. As I take a deep breath in, and then exhale, all the tension my body has been holding onto is released.

5. I have set boundaries in my life that cannot be violated.

6. I know that I am not alone. Many people have been where I am now.

7. Healing is possible for me.

8. I acknowledge that I am ready to never look back.

9. I am breaking a cycle by letting go.

10. If I need healing time now, that is okay, and I can take it.

11. There will be a point in my journey where I will consider myself healed, and I am striving for that point every day.

Trauma

1. I am okay today.

2. I am safe.

3. Today, I will start to build a better life for myself.

4. I will not let my trauma rule my life.

5. My experience may have led to some changes in me, but I can still lead an amazing life.

6. I have the power to leave this behind me.

7. I will seek help on the bad days.

8. I have the right to be my top priority.

9. I was created with great power for self-healing.

10. I am strong and brave.

11. I shouldn't have had to face what I did, but that doesn't mean I'm not capable of overcoming it.

12. I will ensure that I am taking care ofmyself, even on the toughest days.

13. I choose to be myself today.

14. I choose to create peace around myself.

15. I have created a safe environment.

16. Nothing can hurt me now.

17. I do not blame myself for the things that have happened.

18. I didn't do anything wrong.

19. I do not need to feel guilty for what has happened.

20. I should never feel ashamed.

21. My experience will never define who I am as a person.

22. I pay attention to my inner child.

23. I am working with my inner child to heal.

24.
My experience doesn't make me worth less than any othe r person.

25. I am allowed to share my story if I want to. No one can hold me back.

26. No one can force me to share my story. If I don't want to, I don't have to.

27. It's over. I am no longer in that situation.

28. I am strong. The fact that I have made it this far proves that.

Weight Loss

Healthy Weight

1. I love myself, no matter what size I am.

2. I can envision my healthy body.

3. I am moving closer to my goal every day.

4. I use the scale to guide my efforts, but not as the measurement of my progress.

5. I understand that losing fat doesn't always mean that pounds are coming off the scale.

6. I have set my goals.

7. I am motivated to have a healthy body.

8. I accept my body for what it is now.

9. My body type, no matter what it is, is beautiful.

10. I am making the conscious choice to be healthy.

11. I will eat vegetables today.

12. I will eat fruit today.

13. I will exercise today.

14. I am allowed to celebrate meeting my goals, no matterhow small those goals may seem to others.

15. I will not let a setback distract me from my goal.

16. As my body becomes healthier, I will notice positivechanges within it.

17. As my body becomes healthier, so will my mind.

18. I commit to removing junk food from my daily diet.

19. I commit to ensuring that I am eating enough food every day.

20. I know that I can feel confident with the size I am even while I work toward my goals.

21. In the days ahead, I will be extremely grateful that I decided to do this.

22. I am on this mission for myself and my body.

23. I am here to take good care of my body and mind.

24. I will be patient with my body.

25. I am losing the mass I need every single day.

26. I can envision my ideal weight.

27. I am making progress to become fitter and stronger every day.

28. I love my body and I am taking care of it.

29. I will lose this weight and keep it off.

30. I am in charge of my future.

31. I am choosing happiness, health, fulfillment, and contentment with my body right now.

Unhealthy Comparisons

1. I will not compare myself to celebrities.

2. I know that many of the fitness models I see do not have a healthy diet and I do not have to look like them.

3. If I notice that I'm comparing myself to one person too much, I will delete that person from my following list. This comparison is not serving me.

4. If I find myself constantly making unhealthy comparisons to people on social media, I will stop. If I can't stop, I will remove apps or unfollow people and do whatever it takes to free myself.

5. I know that I have a unique body type and that it might not respond the same way to a method as someone else's would.

6. If my friend and I go on the same diet, we both may have different outcomes, although both will be healthy.

7. I will not compare myself to an older version of myself who was able to fit into some clothes better.

8. I will not let others make negative comments about my weight.

9. I will not let comments about my appearance get to me.

10. I understand that weight loss alone will not bring me happiness and a positive body image. I will also give myself the love I need.

11. I am taking the time to nurture my body.

12. I am worth this journey and so is my body.

13. I will succeed in my goal. There is no stopping me.

14. I will lose this weight naturally.

15. I don't need the approval of others to achieve my goal.

16. I accept my body's shape and beauty.

17. Striving for a healthier self does not mean that I don'tlove myself right now.

18. I am great!

19. I feel good about myself.

20. I accept every aspect of who I am.

21. I am excited about my future.

22. I am grateful for my body and everything that it does.

Mindful Eating

1. I eat only when I feel hungry.

2. I am in control of my eating habits.

3. I listen to my body when it talks about food.

4. If my body asks me for food, I will give my body that food.

5. I will ensure that the food is a need and not a craving before I eat it.

6. I will ensure that my eating is balanced every day.

7. I will not restrict what I am eating.

8. Eating with intention satisfies my needs.

9. When I eat dessert, I will do so while practicing mindfulness.

10. I enjoy the taste of healthy food that nourishes my body.

11. I reflect on my food choices to ensure that they are serving me.

12. I do not ignore my hunger when it is there.

13. I eat with a sense of discipline.

14. I let go of my negative past with food.

15. I will no longer allow myself to feel guilty for choices that I may have made in the past, or that I have made recently.

Non-Scale Victories

1. Eating healthy food for a week is a victory.

2. Exercising consistently is a victory.

3. Gaining more energy because of my habits is a victory.

4. Feeling good in the size I am wearing is a victory.

5. I don't need to lose weight every week. Sometimes my victory is simply that I didn't gain anything.

6. I am creating a body that I love, not just a number.

7. I move easier and with more grace.

8. Stopping habits that make me overeat is a victory.

9. I am making decisions now that lead to a better future. That future is my victory.

10. I am reclaiming control of my mind.

Coping With Stress and Emotions Without Food

1. I will not let my emotions rule my food consumption.

2. I will not let a bad day get the best of my health goals.

3. If I have eaten out of emotion in the past, that does not make me a failure, it just means that the time to start is now.

4. I will not overeat today.

5. I have people around me who want me to succeed.

6. There is love out there that I can turn to.

7. There are hobbies that I can turn to.

8. If I feel stressed and emotional, I will look at something nice for myself.

9. If I feel stressed and upset, I can put on my favorite movie.

10. If I have returned to my former eating habits, I have not doomed myself. I know that I can stop at any time.

Sleep

Calm

1. I am calm.

2. I am safe.

3. I am okay.

4. I will not get worked up.

5. I am at ease.

6. I am in a sanctuary for myself.

7. My mind is at ease.

8. My body is ready for rest.

9. My worries are fleeing my brain.

10. My eyes and body are tired and waiting for rest.

11. I am grateful for this amazing bed to sleep in.

12. I love my body, and I will care for it by going to sleep.

Peace of Mind

1. I am at peace.

2. There isn't anything that can get to me now.

3. I have worked hard today and now I know that it is time to rest.

4. I will achieve a sense of peace and serenity as I fall asleep.

5. I have no fears about going to bed.

6. I am ready to wake up and feel refreshed.

7. I am ready to shut my eyes and take a break.

8. I refuse to let fear and anxiety rule my sleep.

9. I will not have a sleepless night.

10. My dreams will be filled with a calming aura.

11. I am completely safe.

12. My stress has no control over me.

13. My worries do not control me.

14. My fears and doubts do not control me.

15. I am letting go so that I can be at peace.

16. I am going to sleep while being at peace with myself.

Letting Go

1. Tomorrow will be a new day. Now, it is time to rest.

2. I will not check my phone tonight.

3. The emails and messages can wait.

4. I will not spend tonight worrying about the things I need to do in the future.

5. I give into my tiredness.

6. I let go of any problems that cross my mind.

7. My dreams are bringing positivity that fills me with hope. I am ready for them.

8. I am choosing sleep over stress.

9. I am choosing sleep over worry.

10. My eyes are closing without me trying.

11. I am heading for a beautiful, undisturbed sleep.

12. By going to sleep, I am preparing my mind for a new perspective.

13. Sleeping is my natural form.

14. My only goal tonight is rest.

15. Every breath I take is bringing me closer to peaceful thoughts.

16. As I sleep, I am being recharged.

17. I am regenerating my mind through sleep. I will behappier tomorrow because of this.

18. I welcome sleep and rest.

Acceptance

1. I am grateful for the relaxed feeling that spreads throughmy body.

2. I did my best today. It is time for me to recharge from doing my best.

3. Tomorrow will bring me a new opportunity that I cannot wait to see.

4. I will enjoy a good night's sleep and wake up with arefreshed outlook.

5. Great things will come after a good night's sleep.

6. I am a beautiful human being and I deserve to rest.

7. My body deserves a full night of sleep.

8. I will stop dwelling on the negative things that are preventing me from sleeping.

9. I am in a natural state of well-being.

10. I accept any mistakes I have made today, but I will not let them define my sleep.

11. I am going to sleep without any anxiety plaguing my mind.

12. I will awaken as my best self tomorrow.

13. I will wake up feeling amazing.

14. I will feel well-rested tomorrow.

15. Tomorrow, I will feel refreshed with my goals in mind.

16. By going to sleep, my body is healing from anything that has happened today.

17. I have given my everything today, and now I must rest so that I have more to give tomorrow.

18. I forgive myself for the mistakes of today, and I resolve to fix them tomorrow.

19. I am allowed to make time for myself to rest.

20. There is nothing more that I can do today.

21. I am giving my future self a gift by going to sleep now.

22. My mind is going to be still.

23. I collect the thoughts and feelings preventing me fromsleep and I release them to the wind.

24. My sleep will leave my body feeling nourished.

25. My sleep will keep me healthy.

26. My bed is a comforting and safe place to rest.

27. I am falling into a deep sleep.

28. My bed is calling me.

29. My bedtime routine is making me sleepy.

30. The only person who needs me right now is myself.

31. I require sleep.

32. I deserve to be able to meet my needs.

33. It has been a long day and my brain is ready for rest.

34. I accept that right now it is time for bed.

35. I cannot serve others, without first serving myself and my needs.

Chapter 5:

Affirmations for Anxiety and Stress

Our lives can be extremely stressful. In today's world, everyone seems to be going at a fast pace. We are constantly working and juggling responsibilities and there never seems to be time to relax. Luckily, there are ways to cope. Sometimes, no matter what is going on around you, it's time to take a step back and breathe.

Anxiety

Managing Anxiety

1. Every day that I get up and out of bed to face the day is a great step forward.

2. I am the strongest person I know.

3. Facing my anxiety makes me strong.

4. I am fighting a battle. Some days I might win and on others, I might lose, but at the end of the day, I am becoming strong.

5. I become stronger with every day that I refuse to give in.

6. I am a wonderful human being.

7. This struggle is real, and I will not let anyone minimize it.

8. Everyone has something hard to deal with in life. For me, it is this and that's okay.

9. Today, I am going to conquer my fears.

10. Today, I choose to accept that I have amazing power.

11. I have a healthy outlet for dealing with my anxiety.

12. I am in touch with my feelings and know when it is time to take a step back.

13. This feeling will not last forever.

14. I will reach out for help in dealing with my anxiety when I need to.

15. I will separate stress related to a specific issue from anxiety.

16. My anxiety stems from stress.

17. My brain is not logically making me anxious. I am simply being reactive to being stressed.

18. When the anxiety hits, I take the time I need to calm down.

19. I keep a peaceful disposition, allowing me to let stress roll off and have no effect.

20. I take the time to allow my mind to rejuvenate to stopthe anxiety.

21. I will make the focus of today be about the things I am grateful for rather than the to-do list.

22. I am choosing confidence in the future and the belief that good things are coming my way.

23. I give myself permission to let go of all my concerns.

24. I am working toward being able to remain peaceful, even under pressure.

25. I am capable of anything I set my mind to.

26. The power of success is within me.

27. I am a mighty force.

28. I refuse to allow the negative comments of others to intrude on how I think about myself.

29. I enter each day without fear.

30. When I say yes to something, it happens as I envision it.

31. I will not let others tear me down.

32. I will not accept negative energy from others. I willonly respond with my own positive persona.

33. I refuse to allow this to get to me.

34. I am more powerful than the self-doubt that lies in my brain.

35. I am made from confidence and others see me as a confident force.

36. I will not let myselfbe disrespected.

37. When I feel anxious, I summon the confidence within me.

38. When I feel upset, I make sure to ground myself in reality.

39. I believe in myself.

40. I am choosing the good energy today and staying awayfrom the bad.

41. I forgive myself for anything bad that has happened in the past.

42. I can see my future clearly.

43. I choose thoughts that nurture my health.

44. I choose thoughts that lead me to positivity.

45. I choose thoughts that allow calm in my day.

46. I am where I'm supposed to be.

47. I choose to spend my energy on my values and not my anxiety.

48. I am identifying triggers.

49. I am focusing on moving one step forward every day.

50. I am not defined by anxiety.

51. Anxiety is not a weakness.

52. I have made it through bad times before.

53. I am growing stronger every day.

54. If I cannot face this alone, that is okay.

Social Anxiety and Panic Attacks

1. I am here for a reason.

2. Family gatherings surround me with people who love me.

3. This is a big event. No one's focus is drawn solely to me.

4. I will speak my presentation clearly today.

5. I will do amazing today.

6. I am not alone in facing this issue. There are many out there like me who also need help.

7. If I need to take a step back during an event, no one can stop me.

8. Allowing myself time in the event to calm down will allow me to return with better focus.

9. If I know I am going to be at an event, I will allow myself ample time before and after the event for self-care and recovery.

10. If the event is big, chances are there is one other person there who feels exactly like me.

11. If I am too overwhelmed by an event, I am allowed to leave.

12. It is not my fault that I feel this way.

13. I am okay.

14. I am strong.

15. This is a temporary state of being.

16. I will overcome this feeling.

17. I know how to breathe.

18. As I inhale, I am taking in air, which contains the calm that I need to sustain myself.

19. I am releasing the anxiety and panic that I feel right now.

20. I am a wonderful and beautiful person.

21. If I need help to calm down, I will seek it.

22. I am powerful and brave, and I will conquer this feeling.

23. If I need to, I can listen to a song to help me calm down.

24. I can do meditation to calm down.

25. I can play a game or draw to calm down.

26. I will calm down in my own time. I will not feel guilty if it takes a while.

27. I am not alone in this experience. There are others outt h e r e who have had the same experience that I am having right now.

28. This issue is temporary.

29. I am going to overcome this problem.

30. This problem is not worth hurting me by stressing about it.

31. I give myself the permission to diveinto this problem with a stress-free mindset.

32. I am capable ofhandling this.

33. If the project is overwhelming, I can help by breaking it down into easier-to-manage sections so that it can be handled better.

34. If there are others putting pressure on me and causing me stress, I will make them step aside so that I can work on this with a calm mindset.

35. Household tasks may feel overwhelming. That is okay.

36. I have a plan with steps in it to help me complete big projects.

Intrusive Thoughts

1. Everyone gets thoughts like this.

2. These thoughts are not my thoughts.

3. I will not entertain these thoughts.

4. I banish these thoughts away from my mind.

5. I will not let thoughts like these take root in my brain.

6. I should never feel bad for thinking these things. My brain has simply created a weird temporary lapse.

7. This thought is the result of a misfire in the brain and nothing more.

8. If I find these thoughts overwhelming, there is help for me to seek.

9. I do not give these thoughts any persuasive power over me.

Stress

Coping With Stressful Situations

1. I allow my brain the time it needs to calm down.

2. I will turn the thoughts off and rid them from my head.

3. I will not allow these thoughts to rule me.

4. When I catch myself overthinking, I will take deep breaths.

5. I can separate myself from my thoughts when needed.

6. I know that the worst thing I think of isn't likely to happen and is only the product of my imagination.

7. I can always let go of my thoughts when I need to.

8. I give myself permission to practice self-care to rid myself of these thoughts

9. I am safe.

10. My brain may get stuck, but I have the power to unstick it.

11. I won't let overthinking interfere with the work I have to do.

12. I can work through my thoughts to find a logical end to this worry.

13. I will not allow this extra stress.

14. This is something I can fight.

15. I will not get swept away in a current of overthinking.

16. I give myself permission to take a break when I need one.

17. Today, I choose not to stress or overthink the things I cannot control.

18. My inner strength is stronger than these thoughts.

19. I will not face today with fear.

20. I remind myself that this event will pass. Eventually, I will not need to stress about it.

21. Even when faced with a challenging task, I can remain calm in both mind and body.

22. I will make life choices that allow me to reduce stress.

23. I will add things into my daily routine that allow me to actively work on stress reduction.

24. I will make changes in my life that lead to less stress in the long run.

25. Others view me as someone calm, peaceful, and able to tackle some of the tough challenges.

26. I have the power to stay in a peaceful state today.

27. I can overcome this state of being.

28. I deserve to be free of this burden.

29. When I start to feel this burden's hold on me rise, I cut it off and do not allow it any further hold.

30. I give myself permission to relax.

31. If I don't finish everything today, it will still be perfectly fine.

32. It's okay for me to step back when I need to.

33. If the stress is overwhelming my ability to do the work, then I will move on to another task.

34. If the stress is coming from not understanding the project, I will reroute my focus and come back later with a fresh set of eyes.

35. It is okay to leave a project unfinished.

36. I know that I may not be able to give my absolute best to every project. If there are too many, then I will need to prioritize and give the bigger ones more attention.

37. I know that I only have so much attention and focus that I can give.

38. I take the time to find the things I am grateful for.

39. I remind myself that this will pass.

40. I am deciding not to let stress rule my life.

41. No matter what time it is or where I am in a project, I can close my eyes and feel a sense of peace.

42. I can focus less on the worries of my mind.

Healthy Coping and Priorities

1. I release this negative energy.

2. I will turn my stress into energy and use it to get things done.

3. When things get overwhelming, I will take a deep breathand remind myself that everything is okay.

4. Each time I submit something or get something done, my stress alleviates.

5. I do not surround myself with stress.

6. When my stress gets overwhelming, I know that it is time to take a break.

7. I maintain care of myself, even when I feel overwhelmed by work.

8. I will not let work stop me from practicing my self-care.

9. I have a naturally calm state.

10. I am stress-free.

11. When I feel overwhelmed with stress, I let my inner peace take over to calm me down.

12. I aim to be an example of peace to others.

13. I replace stress and anxiety with laughter and happiness.

14. I can allow myself to be worry-free.

15. Even when faced with stressful events, I will allow myself the chance to be at peace and relaxed.

16. My mind and my body reach a peaceful state when I am allowing myself the chance to breathe.

17. As I take a deep breath in, my lungs inhale good, clean energy. As I exhale, it will push out the bad energy.

18. Releasing stress is something I naturally do.

19. As time goes by, releasing built-up stress will become easier.

20. As time goes by, releasing stress will act to increase the sense of peace that I feel.

21. I can manage stress by prioritizing the important tasks and saving the smaller ones for later.

22. I know that doing my tasks in a certain order is helpful.

23. I make time for my hobbies and the things that interest me to increase the peace I feel and reduce the stress in my life.

24. Once I complete a task, a portion of my stress will leave with it.

25. I make myself my top priority.

26. I know that if I can't function, then I cannot manage my stress.

27. I make stress relief a priority every single day.

28. I make my mental health a priority every single day.

29. I make time to relax every single day.

30. The time I need to unwind after a long day is naturally there.

31. I have a regular time set up for me to just let go of the stress I am facing.

Positive Thinking

1. I am releasing tension from my body.

2. I refuse to allow negative thoughts into my mind.

3. Once I finish this project, I will feel amazing.

4. I will feel great for accomplishing my goals today.

5. I have done amazing things.

6. I have met my goals each day before, and I will do itagain happily.

7. I have power over what I get done today.

8. I have the power to leave an unfinished project when I need to.

9. I will not allow my life to become overburdened bystressful events and happenings.

10. I will put focus on the things that bring me joy.

11. I will set aside time for activities that allow me to connect with my peaceful self.

12. I will put in the time to ensure that I am living peacefully.

13. Stress does not hold a true purpose in my life.

14. I will not allow myself to be burdened by toxicity any longer.

15. My positivity doesn't leave room for negative thoughts in my head.

16. My inner strength will get me through hard moments.

17. I am invincible and I can do this.

18. I am giving my best at this moment.

19. I am ready to do this.

20. I can take on the challenges I face.

21. I am ready to have a great day.

22. I will face the world with calm and confidence.

23. I am fearless and amazing.

24. If I believe in myself, then I can do what I want.

25. I will continue on.

26. My confidence will carry my journey.

27. I refuse to let my brain wander into worry.

Relaxation

Visualization

1. My relaxed state is natural.

2. When I close my eyes, I can instantly feel relaxed.

3. I take my relaxed self into stressful situations and remain relaxed. This enables me to get more done and do better things on projects.

4. When I feel overwhelmed, I have an image that I can hold onto that allows me to destress.

5. I may be stressed now, but I can see the future ahead of me.

6. My future self will not be stressed or overburdened by worry.

7. I can see myself in a positive state.

8. I can see the energy that I get from relaxing.

9. I accept positive feelings that are heading my way.

10. I am put at ease by an accessible sense of relaxation.

11. When I am overwhelmed, I inhale a sense of relaxation and exhale a sense of stress.

12. I can visualize the life ahead of me that I deserve. It is free of stress and anxiety.

13. When I am overwhelmed, I can stop and visualize all my worries leaving my body.

14. My brain is unwinding itself from tension and stress.

15. I see myself as a happy and positive person that is unburdened by worry.

16. If I find that the space I am in isn't helping my stress levels, I can visualize myself in a different space.

17. I can see the power and peace that radiate off me. I imagine it spreading to others, allowing them to fulfill their goals in the day too.

18. I can visualize my health in its perfect state.

19. When I try to think of perfection, I see myself.

20. I can see the road ahead, and I know what I need for my body to be at peace.

21. I feel at ease.

22. I can sense the world around me relaxing.

23. I can visualize myself letting go of the things that are holding me down.

24. I can identify my struggles and visualize the path to clearing them.

25. I have a place that I can visualize to help me regain focus.

26. I can clearly see what my priorities are right now.

27. I can see the end of the day approaching.

28. I can see when I need to give myself a moment to relax.

29. I can see my next goal right in front of me.

Calm

1. I have a sense of calm to carry with me wherever I go.

2. I have a sense of calm when I am in a situation that feels stressful.

3. I carry a sense of calm with me when I feel that things aren't going the way I want them to.

4. I carry a sense of calm with me when I am dealing with difficult co-workers or clients.

5. I carry a sense of calm with me when it comes to my family. Even when they overreact, I do not give in.

6. I will carry my calm with me and allow it to foster into others.

7. If I am dealing with someone who is very upset, I will remain calm. By doing so, I am fostering calm in them and myself.

8. I will remain calm in the face of deadlines, even as the push for my energy.

9. By choosing to remain calm, I am not devoting extra energy to stress or negativity.

10. Remaining in a calm state of mind is good for my long-term health.

11. By remaining in this calm state, I am keeping my physical body in a stable place.

12. I will allow myself to enter a state of peace.

13. I deserve a calm state of mind and body.

14. When I feel anxious, I can imagine a sense of calm gently setting over me.

15. I am unwavering in my sense of calm.

16. I push my calm toward others to allow them the sense that I feel.

17. I am grateful for my sense of calm and its ability to help my day.

18. I am grateful for the impact that being calm has made, and will continue to make, on my life.

19. I make ample time each day for activities that will foster calm.

20. My sense of calm is not a facade that I show others. It is deep in my spirit too.

21. If I feel my calm start to be overtaken by stress, I have tools to help bring me back into my reality.

22. I will only deal with others when I know I can do so calmly.

23. My sense of calm has a strong foundation. It cannot easily be built over in any way.

24. Even when faced with dire situations, I will let my calm emotions precede me.

25. By remaining calm, I am allowing my brain to think of the best possible rational solutions.

26. By remaining in a state of mind that lets me think, I am coming up with the best possible solutions.

27. My calm lets me be a better thinker.

28. My calm allows me to give my ideas the merit they deserve.

29. My calm allows me to be more creative.

30. My calm will allow me to do great things.

31. My calm will let me become someone great.

32. My calm will allow me to think outside the box.

33. Being calm makes me stronger.

34. By carrying a calm attitude, I am giving myself more energy.

35. I promise myself I will be gentle when it comes to me.

36. My sense of calm is natural.

37. I am practicing and perfecting my sense of calm every day.

38. I am building skills by practicing calm.

39. If I lose control and become worked up, I will return to my calm.

40. I will not let others upset the balance of calm that I carry within me.

41. I will not overwork myself to the point of disturbing the state of calm I have.

Self-Care

1. I take time for self-care.

2. I allow self-care to relax me and make me feel amazing.

3. I practice self-care to remind myself that no matter what happens outside the walls of my home, the inside is still filled with the good energy I choose to have.

4. I will practice self-care, even when it seems impractical to a deadline.

5. My self-care can look like anything that relaxes me. I can soak in a bath, paint a picture, go on a run, or do whatever I need to feel like myself again.

6. I will practice self-care, even if others say that it's silly.

7. In my time with self-care, I will rejuvenate myself.

8. I cannot handle the outside world unless I take care of myself first.

9. I will practice self-care today by paying attention to my health.

10. I will practice self-care by saying no when I cannot do something and not budging on that decision.

11. I will practice self-care by enjoying my favorite morning beverage.

12. If I know that a day is going to be stressful, I have time carved out immediately afterward for self-care and relaxation.

13. I deserve self-care and to make time for self-care. No one can tell me otherwise.

14. Self-care is essential to my health and well-being.

15. I will not let someone interfere with my self-care.

16. To take care of others, I need to be at my strongest.

17. The healing powers of self-care transcend onto me and make me feel amazing.

18. Self-care has the power to wash all my stress away.

19. Self-care for me might not look the same way it does for my friend. The goal is to do something that regenerates my mind and body.

20. I am a beautiful creature and caring for myself on a deep level will reflect that.

21. Practicing self-care does not make me weak. It allows me to become stronger in many ways.

22. Self-care is a need. Therefore, it is in place before people's wants.

23. Self-care practices last however long I need them to.

24. I can go out for an event for self-care.

25. I can stay in and spend time with myself for self-care.

26. I give myself permission to set aside my work in favor of self-care.

27. I will create my space for self-care.

28. I will practice self-care even if it has been a good day.

29. I will take breaks when I need to.

30. I listen to my body when it tells me to take a break.

Sleep When Stressed

Calm

1. My mind is at ease.

2. I am mentally ready to go to sleep.

3. I do not feel anxious.

4. I do not feel burdened by worry.

5. I am carrying calm energy to bed.

6. My stress is melting away.

7. I am free of worry.

8. Being calm will carry me to sleep.

9. I am entering a deep sleep.

10. I am going into a space where I cannot be disturbed.

11. I am going into a trance. Here, I will rest.

12. My brain is emptying of the worries from today.

13. My eyes are naturally closing as I prepare to sleep.

14. My arms and legs are releasing tension as my body drifts off.

15. I am letting go of the tension I feel in my back as I go to sleep.

16. I am emotionally ready to turn off the lights.

17. I will not worry if I cannot fall asleep right away.

18. I am easing into rest blissfully.

19. I am becoming more and more relaxed.

20. If I cannot fall asleep right away, I will keep my sense of calm.

Peace of Mind

1. I am safe and secure.

2. I no longer need to worry about the events of today.

3. Tomorrow's problems can wait.

4. I am at peace with the good and bad things that cameabout today.

5. If something bad has happened today it can be fixed tomorrow.

6. I deserve my time to rest.

7. I am grateful for the good things that happened today.

8. I am grateful for the lessons I have learned today.

9. I am grateful for the happiness and the love that Ihave experienced today.

10. I am happy that it is time to relax.

11. I am ready to enter the world of dreams.

12. I feel relaxed and at ease.

13. I am not carrying any negative energy to bed with me.

14. I am ready to fall into a peaceful state.

15. By reaching a peaceful state, I am guaranteeing that I will feel refreshed for tomorrow.

16. I have set aside my doubts from the day.

17. I feel content with the world.

18. I am ready for sleep.

19. I do not have any other priorities right now.

20. Worry does not exist for me.

Letting Go

1. I will not let my anxiety stop me from sleeping.

2. I am ready to go to sleep.

3. I do not owe today any more thought.

4. My problems can be resolved tomorrow.

5. I cannot fix things tonight.

6. By going to bed, I am setting myself up for better things.

7. I will not wake up to anything related to work or school.

8. I forgive those who have caused me problems today.

9. I let go of my worry and anxiety.

10. I let go of my responsibilities. They are not importantright now.

11. I will not entertain the worries of the future.

12. I am letting go now so that I might be in themoment tomorrow.

13. I am slipping into unconsciousness.

14. I am not holding onto negative thoughts.

15.
I am ridding myself of anything that is acting to keep m e awake.

16. I permit myself to forget about the issues of today. Theyare going to be there to handle them tomorrow.

17. I will rest fully and beautifully.

18. I am at ease.

19. I am disconnecting from the worries of the world.

20. My only concern now is sleep.

Breathing

1. My breath is calm.

2. My breath is even.

3. My breath is steady.

4. I am settled into a routine breathing pattern.

5. My breathing is preparing my brain for sleep.

6. My breathing is powerful.

7. My breathing will carry me into sleep.

8. I am inhaling the calm, relaxed, air, and exhaling any anxiety and stress so that it no longer holds power over me.

9. If I struggle to fall asleep, I will focus on my breathing instead of my worries.

10. As my breathing evens out, I am joining the world around me in taking part in time for rest.

11. I do not need to worry about anything else.

12. My breathing is carrying life through me as I sleep.

13. My breath travels through my body, relaxing it for sleep.

14. My breath brings me into the next morning.

15. I accept the wondrous power of my lungs and their ability to do what I need them to.

16. When I am inhaling, I am continuing the restful cyclewithin my body.

17. My breath is providing my body with the resources it needs for me to sleep.

18. My breath will be with me while I sleep.

19. I can count my breaths to help me sleep.

20. I can feel peace and drowsiness come to me as I breathe.

Acceptance

1. I accept the incoming drowsiness.

2. I accept the events of today.

3. I accept the gift of sleep.

4. I accept that it is time to go to bed.

5. I accept that I cannot change the past.

6. I accept that my work for the day is done.

7. I accept my bed and pillows, and the comforts I have.

8. I accept the love I have received.

9. I accept that I am tired.

10. I accept that, as a human, I need rest.

11. I will not continue working too hard.

12. I accept that I need to go to sleep to help recharge for the next day.

13. I accept the gifts I have received today.

14. I accept the promise of tomorrow.

15. I accept the limits of my body.

16. I accept the moon in the sky and its signal for all to rest.

17. I am ready to go to bed tonight.

18. I am ready to face tomorrow.

19. I accept the ability to wake up to a new day.

20. I accept the calm and the peace, and I am ready to move forward.

References

Abundance No Limits. (n.d.). *70 positive relationship affirmations that work fast*. *Abundance* No Limits. https://www.abundancenolimits.com/relationship-affirmations/

Cartwright, D. (2021, January 29). *Easy confidence affirmations for success that really Work*. The Daily Shifts. https://www.thedailyshifts.com/blog/easy-confidence-affirmations-for-success-that-really-work

Cervino, S. (2020, April 17). *20 positive affirmations for well-being*. Sivana East. https://blog.sivanaspirit.com/mf-gn-positive-affirmations-wellbeing/

Chrissy. (2020, October 13). *75 powerful affirmations for self-love*. Fun Loving Families. https://www.funlovingfamilies.com/affirmations-for-self-love/

Darley, D. (2021, April 22). *101 positive affirmations - curiosity*. https://daledarley.com/101-positive-affirmations-curiosity/

Davis, R. (2012, February 4). *49 growth affirmations*. The Affirmation Spot Blog. https://affirmationspot.me/2012/02/04/49-growth-affirmations/

Horton, C. (2021, September 22). *87 positive affirmations for self-love*. Clever Girl Finance.

https://www.clevergirlfinance.com/blog/loving-affirmations-for-self-love/

Indeed Editorial Team. (2021, January 4). *Positive Affirmations in the workplace: Impact, tips and examples.* Indeed Career Guide. https://www.indeed.com/career-advice/career-development/positive-affirmations

Killoren, C. (2021, February 27). *Life, love and relationships: 50 positive affirmations for daily life.* Relish. https://hellorelish.com/articles/daily-positive-affirmations.html

Kristenson, S. (2020, November 7). *45 healing affirmations for your mind, body, and soul.* Happier Human. https://www.happierhuman.com/healing-affirmations/

Luke. (n.d.). *50 self-esteem affirmations [Repeat them daily to build self-worth].* Thrive Global. https://thriveglobal.com/stories/50-self-esteem-affirmations-repeat-them-daily-to-build-self-worth/

Logue, B. (n.d.). *120 positive affirmations for health & healing.* The Daily Positive. https://www.thedailypositive.com/120-positive-affirmations-for-health-and-healing/

Mike. (2020, February 21). *Positive thinking affirmations.* Positive Thinking Mind. https://positivethinkingmind.com/positive-thinking-affirmations/

Pangilinan, J. (2021, February 25). *35 relationship affirmations to grow your love together.* Happier Human. https://www.happierhuman.com/relationship-affirmations/

Prancier, L. R. V. (n.d.). *30 positive sleep affirmations to relax at night!* PRANCIER. https://prancier.com/blog/positive-sleep-affirmations

Rodriguez, L.H. (n.d.). *20 positive affirmations for confidence and self-esteem.* Lucilehr.com. https://www.lucilehr.com/blog/20-positive-affirmations-for-confidence-and-self-esteem

Sarah. (2020, May 29). *35 positive affirmations for health and wellness.* A Simple and Contented Life. https://asimpleandcontentedlife.com/positive-affirmations-health-wellness/

Sarros, K. (n.d.). *20 affirmations to boost happiness and confidence at work.* Kailyn Sarros. https://www.kailynsarros.com/blog/20-affirmations-to-boost-happiness-and-confidence-at-work

Scott, E. (2020, October 28). *How to use positive affirmations for stress relief.* Verywell Mind. https://www.verywellmind.com/how-positive-affirmations-help-manage-stress-3144814

Stefanie. (2017, April 24). *25 affirmations for resilience.* The Focus on You. http://thefocusonyou.com/2625-2/

Taylor. (2020, August 10). *51 self-love affirmations to feel & attract more love.* Taylor's Tracks. https://www.taylorstracks.com/self-love-affirmations/

Thompson, F.M. (2020, August 17). *Self-love: 50 positive affirmations for depression.* As the Bird Flies. https://www.asthebirdfliesblog.com/posts/positive-affirmations-for-depression

Ursano, I. (2021, January 3). *30 daily affirmations for success (and 3 ways to make them work!).* Women Blazing Trails. https://womenblazingtrails.com/daily-affirmations-for-success-that-work/

Wallace, D. (2019, August 7). *25 positive affirmations to improve your mindset.* Positivity Post. https://medium.com/positivity-post/25-positive-affirmations-to-improve-your-mindset-438377b03009

Wendy. (2021, March 3). *40+ inspiring positive affirmations for friends and friendship.* Life & Business with Wendy. https://lifeandbusinesswithwendy.com/affirmations-for-friends/

Williamson, J. (2017, July 24). *20 gratitude affirmations for deep happiness & hope for the future.* Healing Brave. https://healingbrave.com/blogs/all/gratitude-affirmations-happiness-hope

www.ingramcontent.com/pod-product-compliance
Ingram Content Group UK Ltd.
Pitfield, Milton Keynes, MK11 3LW, UK
UKHW021321270725
7091UKWH00025B/309